無用な才能百科事典

INTRODUCTION

What is "Michael Chang?" Mouthy seduction, cocky disrespect. A trickster fox, a blazing blur, a queer and giddy wordplay.

"Michael Chang" is your avatar traversing 2022's writhingly dense networks of desire: steamy live gym bodies and frat boys, the bonds of blow jobs, electronic blasts algorithmically personalized, the Narcissus mirror of the phone screen, the suck of it.

To desire. To be desired. Almanac considers such matters from all angles at a bitchy distance, but can never get above it all, it is ever also implicated. It whips, snaps from line to line so fast you'll miss things: high craft, deep play.

Youth, beauty, art world, poetry world, gender, race, fashion, celebrity, hookups, Azn mystique, "Michael Chang" is tricking through, beguiled, intrigued, amused by these realms. What would Warhol do as a queer Azn? Is the sassy braggadocio an armor which obfuscates some tiny heart of true longing, true love? The poetry slips through and makes you feel silly for asking the question.

"Michael Chang" hovers at a distance, vibrates with Euphoria, Shahid Ali, JT LeRoy, Spicer, Warhol. Just try and pin that name down, or try to fix in place the mysterious "Blake."

Enter the pleasure of pursuit as you are already pursued. "Michael Chang" slips away into the tangles, like the sly coyote. Left behind, in the clearing, are these poems like a forbidden stash of queer bottle rockets, ready for reader to sparkle and blow.

—Jason Zuzga

PRAISE FOR MICHAEL CHANG'S ALMANAC OF USELESS TALENTS

In case your motto is "If you don't have anything nice to say, come sit by me," save a seat for Michael Chang's Almanac of Useless Talents. Irreverent, immediate, and delectably shady, Chang's poems spare no one, whether they're clocking celebrities or exes or poets (who all pretty much deserve it). This book isn't just a whirlwind of spirited invective, although I'd still be fully entertained if it were, given how deftly Chang works in that mode. Look closer and you'll find moments of tenderness and vulnerability too: "Honesty is not a special place / But you would be there with me, finally."
—Mark Bibbins

Here comes Michael Chang's superb Almanac of Useless Talents, sampling from our absurd and dangerous zeitgeist, daring you to say "poetry shouldn't talk like that" (or about that), hilariously insulting to various po- and show-biz celebrities, withering about white people's antics, journeying way beyond "sex positive" into a territory where sex is ubiquitous, omnivorous, fun(ny) (sometimes), ridiculous (often)—but still here, as in the old poetry about desire, not getting what one wants in the way one wants is a frequent source of pain. Radically non-dual—praising the most solicitous lover, who turns out to be Satan—and "Always remembering not to give a damn," Chang pulls the rug out from under sublimity, but equally from irony. If I'd had access to this wise book when I was 10, I would have been happier, and queerer, quicker.
—Patrick Donnelly

Michael Chang's poetry collections are praised for their biting wit and humor, for their critique of injustice, for their juxtaposition of highbrow and low, for their velocity, their leaps, their sense of scale, for their sweeping range of style and subject and tone. The praise is well-earned and accurately describes Chang's newest book, Almanac of Useless Talents. With stinging banter and righteous indignation, Chang calls out a system rigged against queerness, against people of color, drawing desire's obsessive nature and its inevitable pain into sharp focus. Chang reminds us that the bawdy, the blunt, the quip are as much a part of poetry as the romantic, the eloquent, the aphoristic. Chang's poems inspire us to critique what we love, not in spite of that love, but because of it.
—Blas Falconer

Overflowing with sass and razorsharp attitude, Michael Chang's Almanac of Useless Talents sashays on the runway into a whirlwind world that's part bacchanal, literary carousel, interrogation, TMZ, court proceeding, and carnival with a cast of plenty: Azns, "white ppl & their holiday stories," and boys, boys, boys as lovelorn love objects. If only dissatisfaction, jealousy, comeuppance, glee, and ennui can more often be rendered this decadently delicious!
—Joseph O. Legaspi

An almanac, yes, but also a camp catalogue, a queer inventory, meteoric in its pace and opulence. It's less of a reading experience and more of a dazzling trajectory. Buckle up.
 —Angelo Nikolopoulos

Michael Chang writes, "have to warn u tho / i kiss & tell," and Almanac of Useless Talents proves that confession true. In this wonderfully horny book, Chang braids self-deprecation and self-confidence into short, sharp, and playful poems on sex, asianness, romance, pop culture, and queenery. In this book, we see a performance of fierce pride and the demand for the reader to submit to Chang's will. But we also see, in all of these poems, a more subdued, more urgent request: so, can we be friends now?
—Gabriel Ojeda-Sagué

Take a multitude of hyperkinetic punchlines, excise all connective tissue, ("Most poems should be no words / Most poems too long & too explainy"), and all the old news images like horseshoe crabs, bone dust, and marrow, then "suck & fuck / shop like Michael Jackson," and caffeinate until its "little bunny heart is pounding," and you'll have something resembling Michael Chang's breakneck masterpiece Almanac of Useless Talents. I love Chang's lexicon of text abbreviations, Chinese characters, smiley faces, and pop culture frippery which seed and aerate the undercurrent of lyric yearning with spontaneous typographic mini-bombs. Romanticism is blown up, as is romance—"you said all of our love, could fit in a tiffany box, you meant this in a good way, i said so can a turd." Beneath the delicious judginess and the literary criticism delivered with the energy of gossip is a foundation of political and literary acuity, rage, yes, and yes, pain, but in a dismal time, this book refuses to be dismal. "Every day I live in fear of being misidentified as another Azn poet but then I realize there's no one like me," Chang writes, and it's true. The ferocious brag is real, and it's a helluva pushback on the forces of disappearance.
—Diane Seuss

Michael Chang's poems are unstoppable, electric, and hyper-energetic. Almanac of Useless Talents is delightful and humorous, crafted with Chang's unique way of queering languages, cultures, and literary tradition.
—Nicholas Wong

MICHAEL CHANG
**ALMANAC OF
USELESS TALENTS**

Silly girls your heads full of boys.

— *John Ashbery*

Terrible sting, terrible storm / I can tell you.

— *Sufjan Stevens*

TABLE OF CONTENTS

NO NO ZONE

if i were that kind of poet

i would tell you abt this marvel of a boy

reliable like the planets

if i were that kind of poet

i would talk abt the twink & his crystal collection

abandoned after his break-up with zachary quinto

if i were that kind of poet

i would admit i don't like to suck but like it when you ask

you're welcome as asbestos lead chips

h.d. as sea monster in christian lacroix

she was so ahead of her time h.d. stands for high definition

bumming cigarettes—looking hot

i ask the greyhound driver abt the shadiest shit he's seen

gas station pay you to pump there

pour things quickly if you don't want to spill

products with fragrance irritate the skin

your little habits are so cute

i watch you nibble on chicken nuggets, you look like those fishies that love dead skin

i've lost my souvenir pennies, want to show you how nice my sheets smell

you hate absence, tab your books

if i followed them would i learn your <3

your existence makes me happy

shorter boys have kinder faces

NATIONAL OCEANIC & ATMOSPHERIC ADMINISTRATION

...

If I wanted to complain, I would complain abt your secrecy,
your big mouth, your lack of gifts,
how you are so annoying, so earnest

...

We don't need to talk—
I just want to be in the same space as you

...

There is a very specific place I want to show you
If you don't agree to come, I'll be sad for at least several hours
Honesty is not a special place
But you would be there with me, finally

...

VAMPIRE WEEKEND IS NOT MY FAVORITE BAND, I SWEAR

charlemagne was a she   wu-tang is a form of chinese

i want to stop expecting you to love / act the way i do

you: on my tongue, fat & meaty like an oyster   i'll make you gasp, your eyes flit & flutter

want not a tin house   much prefer a white castle

i'm the kind of girl to pick purple orchids   buy wine in bulk

i had an ex, her name was chow chow   indonesian heiress, she was something else

word on the street is grasshopper   word from the front lines is resist

gave a lot up for this country   all i got was an everything bagel

what is it with poets & horseshoe crabs?   can't even eat them

i'm vegan but i'd cook them in butter just for fun   that'd be a hoot

what the fuck is ron padgett even going on abt?   has anyone more caucasian ever existed?

i picture ron padgett whenever someone says "victim of a crime"

sorry to be so glib, boy in flannel shirt   make these daffodils bloom brown & yellow

don't dilly-dally, now-boyfriend shirt   i'll be your crash dummy, i know you love to pretend

practice your kissing on me,   show off your tongue & that amazing reach

fill me like a pit   from here to LAX

i could act like i spent a lot of time on this poem,   talk abt forms & vessels & bodies

but we know that's bullshit   so do me a solid,   mei-mei bersssenbrugge

i've seen your browser history & taste for alternadudes,   give up the name of your supplier

i don't have all day,   blade-thin boys are waiting for me   we can talk compassion later

we're gonna put an elephant in a dress   sit her down, give her a steak sandwich

extra ketchup   or what have you

ALMANAC OF USELESS TALENTS

"Blake sits naked in his garden"—Anne Waldman

•

1. Always keeping your white shirts spotless & clean

2. Always remembering your dreams

3. Always remembering not to give a damn

4. Always plotting the most efficient route to any destination

5. Always recalling the hours of operation of any store

6. Always avoiding being bored by white ppl & their holiday stories

7. Always identifying the exact species of eel

8. Always identifying the exact chemical composition of any object

9. Always identifying a bottle's vintage & country of origin

10. Always knowing where the nearest wine-opener is

11. Always knowing if something is genuine or pleather

12. Always knowing if someone believes in God—you know—truly

13. Always distinguishing between Iraq & Iran, Obama & Osama

14. Always differentiating between ppl of a different race—correctly—5 minutes too late

15. Always recalling the plot of every rom-com made after 1980 with scientific precision

16. Always knowing what's lurking in the water or in the dark

17. Always knowing if someone is the Reverend Al Sharpton

18. Always knowing where someone went to school & if it was Harvard

19. Always being able to tell a boy's dick size & whether he knows how to use it

20. Always being able to get any boy named _____ (or, in the alternative, _____)

21. Always being able to make him stay

FAST

"Over 200 dogs saved from dog meat trade & abuse set to fly to new homes in the U.S."
—People magazine headline

•

a wicked woman used to laugh at me for reading vogue

she had butt ugly clothes—she is dead now

amateur word magician

laughs lie in the fuck-ups

tasty pooches

tell them we want it extra spice

fire up the hotpot

bring forth the chili sauce

get dat yin-yang broth right

ur chicken—my sea

i've always wanted to own a shawarma stand

unlimited fries & hot rotating meat

so random & hot

dat anonymous solace

door dat don't exist

there are no sacred cows—only scared sheep

jimmy don't play with ur food

beat ur sexy meat

dat lupine milk

a cutting knife

nice boys—

boys who think they're nice boys—

nice enough boys—

the respectability of it all

u walk on water but i'd rather swim

woof! u ugly in this light

没你我没差 FINE W/O U DIPTYCH

my uneasy king

make ur bulb glow for me

with u i can't make my voice cruel

altho u deserve it

& i hate the word *deserve*

— — —

u are planet i am space junk

thought i was a missile

seeking ur heat but i was blowing myself up

i am but a jester in ur court

call me from some loud place

call u encyclopedia brown cuz u have me figured out

compliment my extraterrestrial hotness

get in there

let ur tongue go forzando

fluffy mashed potato

none of dat sweet shit either

ur summer's milk

my soft & wet

have to warn u tho

i kiss & tell

加州一夜情 CALIFORNIA ONE NIGHT STAND

▲

In Venice I meet a guy who sounds exactly like Seth Rogen except he is Azn
I learn that he grew up with a debilitating speech impediment
He learned how to speak from watching Seth Rogen movies
One day, totally unfeeling, he says *show me your hole*
He looks up, expression blank, as if he'd said *please pass the salt*
You're an incorrigible flirt, I giggle
After meaningful sex, he shakes me awake,
says *don't forget my preserves from Zabar's*
I notice he's thrown my wallet away,
replaced it with a new Cartier
I am different now: I have a Spotify, my foam has memory

▲

别说我LOCAL   别说我没用

别说我心狠手辣   忘记你我做不到

▲

for me the highest praise is saying ur poem is for smart ppl
i write gutter poetry
for dirty minds

ur poems make me feel swaddled in finest velvet
engulfed in scholarly love
it's gentle, recalling words like *curvature* & *slope*

time to kiss

▲

i ask a magazine abt submitting to them
they reply right away, say *how abt, just maybe,*
we submit to you

500 HORSES OUTSIDE AT THE VALET

"*We wrote our own destiny / in parking lots & empty streets*"—Thomas Rhett

"*Just keep heading towards anything that ain't me*"—Chris Lane

•

Don't talk to me abt pretty privilege
All I know is ugly condemnation

You say
STEP ASIDE NATHAN LANE WE HAVE A NEW THEATRICAL KWEEN

I say
ARE YOU WEARING THOSE SHORTS I LIKE

You the hungry caterpillar
burrowing in
making space for yourself
How inconsiderate

Bowery smasher
Subway slasher
Stop! in the name of love
We don't often come face-to-face with a monster

You need to be pet like kitty
You don't care who does it
Who even are you
You're a Xerox of a Xerox of a fax

When I show you the clip of the Azn & the white (not a porno)
You assume I am the Azn
I say did you just typecast me as the Azn
You say *no I typecast you as the tiger on the loose*

Astral meaning reminiscent of your magnificent ass
Boy who cried wolf just wants some pie
Are you gonna give it
Nom nom nom

AWFUL GHOSTS

Have you ever had steak / with a boy named Blake / have you / with a dinner spoon / what / no / me neither / I always bring it / up to my lips / in worship

*

You hold hand with Spanish girl / big cow eye / I refute her / swat her away / shoo shoo / like fly

*

Don't customarily write poems for fuccbois / but here you go / piss on it with your attractive penis / *my penis is tiny but mighty* / well baby that's half true / excuses one after another / human centipede

*

I just want to love & live / suck & fuck / shop like Michael Jackson / buy shit I don't need / more books of terrible poetry / will you please stop saying "incantation" / let's dance

*

Come into my office / "office" meaning bed / do you get it / my bed my office / my office my bed

*

They say the water is sweeter in Japan / don't know if this is true / there's no place I'd rather drown

*

you → o ← butthole

ghastly / to be nibbled / like bacon bits / why do I want it all the time

CARNAL FLOWER

u vegetable

u come from dirt

u smell like sheep

i'm tired of ur stinky prison

i found the porn version of u, his eyes flat & blue

pigeon chest, with a much bigger tool

he treats me right, makes me hot chai, knows better than to call it "chai tea"

runs out for non-dairy ice cream, remembers coffee is my favorite

wraps me in a blanket with sensitive native insignia

frowns upon senseless state-sponsored violence

appropriately criticizes drones & detention

doesn't proselytize or allegorize or deify

shields my eyes from roadkill

holds his long, tan arm out when the car comes to an abrupt stop

his motto is c'est la vie, he practices no judgment

means what he says, most of the time

he takes me thru foothills, leads me thru valleys

knows the difference between the hudson & east rivers

trawls me like the river's bottom

always checks if i'm comfortable, sees if i want to trade places

when he looks at me he sees only love

yes, he's a catch, he's perfection

satan is just the name he goes by

THAT NIGHT IN THE STABLES

solemn like informants

his nose buried in my neck

the fumes we inhaled

my eyes drowsy

pinched together in hurt

his golden thing like hot metal

hidden to the hilt

his curls in my bite

honeyed wood shavings

salt on his brow just a speck

we were no relation

then he was mine

i don't recall what came next

but he definitely stepped in it

干爹 DADDY

lie to me like the last japanese soldier

u are dynamite stick i am loose lighter

wuz ur movie boondock saints

wuz ur kink debt forgiveness

i like ur time zone

run roughshod over me

yea touch me an hour in the future

what did i say abt being too tender

what did u say abt biting the hand that feeds

how those who can't (teach)

secret me in (what will the neighbors say)

u've mistaken me for someone who cares

realistically i have forgotten u (department of forgotten affairs)

this is not a drill

PERSON OF INTEREST

山旮旯 or *san ka la*—a cantonese phrase meaning a place in the middle of nowhere

that's where we met

千里眼 & 顺风耳 are two folkloric figures in china—together they're unstoppable

顺风耳 can hear the subtlest of sounds, carried over great distances by the wind

i'll be discreet, the coast is clear

千里眼 can see over great distances, span thousands of 里

confuse oresteia with osteria, smooth me over royal jelly

a 里 is a unit of measurement also found in korea & japan

conquer me royal navy, come here my possibility tuna

a metaphor for an impossible distance is 十万八千里 (108000里)

state college is an hour & a half from harrisburg. that's the distance i would go for you. you drove

5 hours to see your ex

in mandarin, *li* (里) sounds like *li you* (理由)—or reason

a commie obsessed with me, commie eye candy, who wudda thought

给我一个理由忘记

hey, low sperm count

kiss me open mouth, swift like taylor

the critics have spoken: *i'd rather be alone than settle for the bare minimum*

rejecting you seems like the easiest thing in the world (you want to be discarded)

you play too much but seduction is a game for two

i hope one day , we are merit ,

young buck , home skillet ,

PRETTY TRAITORS DRINK TOPO CHICO

u taste amazing i mean u have amazing taste

ur a nice boy cuz u could've called ross ugly but didn't

(he is truly ugly)

a truck-stop lychee martini

jersey ppl don't even pump their own gas

guess i knew u were an all lowercase kind of guy

^^^^jenny zhang said that

(shocker) u get around

i want to gift u wit poetry books no one reads

i want us to have skin-to-skin contact

that hum of corrupt flesh

spin me round michelle kwan

pissing contest & ur not winning

ur brain smooth like back of dolphin

get drunk sick swan on the subway

call me senpai

had a teacher wit a guy laroche purse

i said sup

she knew i was the most winningest azn

my stage name is debussy for a reason

nosy white girl says *hey u travel light*

i say *all i need is right here* & point down

(my other suitcase)

am i ur hero yet

never impregnate ur heroes

don't threaten me wit a good time

have u been nominated for high office

have u noticed that i stopped calling u baby

billy milligan it so i can disappear into the woods

experience falling for u again & again

SAD BOY PUBLIC RELATIONS

1. CONSISTENCY

u type immaculate to me—do u hate me

2. NONCHALANCE

untangle urself for a moment & cheer me up

3. CHARM

ur prodigious
a savant
ur gf's so dumb she thinks contemporary music means the beatles

4. DRINKING

u obfuscate
cling onto flimsy girl

5. EFFORTLESSNESS

i kiss two fingers pinched together
pretend it is u

6. ATHLETICISM

the closest u got to sports was athlete's foot
i feel u hard as pear

7. DISCIPLINE

hold me down
tell me u don't like boy

8. PUBLIC SPIRITEDNESS

seel me like a hawk
i can be tame if u give me what i want

对号入座 TAKE A SEAT

"Above all else, guard your heart, for everything you do flows from it"—Proverbs 4:23

●

ur cute   ur mother must've been beautiful

      want to 陪你淋雨
      (why didn't she raise u right)

               十个他不如一个你   u mess me up
                                 (punch ur own ticket & go)

●

once upon a time i said i wanted to download you onto a thumb drive but it now occurs to me that i would still need time to look thru those files so i guess the new line is i wish i could inject you directly into my veins i can't tell if your confidence is an act i love that i miss all the signs i love that i am bad at love where did you come from 来路不明 by some fluke some quirk of circumstance we met but we are 天差地别 you listen to artists i've never heard of i love your limbs what you call your bony body are the things you say part of some elaborate plot why did you tell me abt your average size your predilection for cheating you said there is a single girl you never cheated on everyone else was SOL does that disqualify me i will appeal i wish i knew where i stood with you are you just using me do you want to be friends with benefits more should we 翻牌 it would shatter me if you said you weren't into me if you didn't find me sexually attractive maybe we should 一刀两断 k says that would be better for my heart that i should always protect my heart you say outrageous things designed i think to push me to the brink but instead the charade pulls me closer believe it or not i seem to be a bat signal for insecure men i hate how songs are slow how they are sad 走投无路 i hate you but you know what i met someone like you today (nevermind)

LEAVE U ON RED

In this dreamy grotto

corn chowder in a bowl

Are you terrifying b/c you are perfect

or perfect b/c you are terrifying

Take a screenshot of what I said

To remind yourself exactly what you are

Panther in a cage

You say things that make ppl forget

Unwitting they come closer

O my

What big hands you have

You take a swipe

Practice your falsetto

O my

What big teeth you have

Pussy willow

Be in my movie

I'll mess up my lines

Screw up the make-believe

So I can kiss you again & again

Yes

I want to smell heavenly

Please gamble responsibly

BLEU DE CHANEL

Sweet Nick, so golden. You learn what *les papillons* means & keep repeating the phrase to anyone who will listen, which is everyone, because you are cute. Every story of yours ends in *& then they fought*

Not hearing from you arouses a feeling in me so monstrous. I rush to tamp it down like the first sign of a spark

You glare so hard, impersonal voice outlining a prognosis, bottomless bitter tonic, I know I must disgust you

It's strange to pick up a book from long ago, say from the 1950s, & see so evidently that their preoccupations were mostly the same as ours, that we are not so special, perhaps even common

The YSL grounds in Marrakesh can be privately toured for a donation of $2,400. There is no other way to access the grounds. No photography is permitted. How cruel, to subject such beautiful gardens to the impermanence of memory, the fleeting nature of perception, the little sensory scraps we manage to hoard like old newspapers & kitty litter

Instead of silence I imagine some blow-up, any plausible explanation, however meager, for the suddenness & cruelty of our disassociation or, more aptly, my abandonment

I've had so much caffeine my little bunny heart is pounding & my body's not reacting well to your absence. The palpitations are translating into an otherworldly experience, transporting me somewhere, far away from you

雪中红 RED IN SNOW

*   *   *

An afterthought . . .
last fry in the bag . . .

*   *   *

Being with you . . .
grief punctuated by sweet nothings . . .

*   *   *

Can you keep up . . .
is this what you wanted . . .

ZERO

•

Decades ago, then-Director of Central Intelligence Roscoe Hillenkoetter testified before Congress on why "homosexuals or other moral perverts" should not serve in positions of public trust.

This bigotry quickly spread to the entirety of the federal government & became official United States policy.

Heterosexuality is so brazen.

•

I. Homosexuals experience emotions "as strong and in fact actually stronger" than heterosexual emotions.

2006 & you're still skinny. You don't show up at camp. We go to Dairy Queen for vanilla soft serve

II. Homosexuals are susceptible "to domination by aggressive personalities."

You say *take risks with your writing* but write abt Sunday roasts & farmers markets. I steal your vodka

III. Homosexuals have "psychopathic tendencies which affect the soundness of their judgment, physical cowardice, susceptibility to pressure, and general instability, thus making a pervert vulnerable in many ways."

Blowhard boasts abt being recruited by the CIA right out of college. "Aren't you a fag?" someone says. Blowhard stops in his tracks, considers his gay partner, his gay chickens, his gay life. He sheds a tear

IV. Homosexuals "invariably express considerable concern" about concealing their condition.

You like Snoopy & I don't know why. We've had a good run, 10 years. We hope for better things

V. Homosexuals are "promiscuous" and often visit "various hangouts of his brethren," marking "a definite similarity to other illegal groups such as criminals, smugglers, black-marketeers, dope addicts, and so forth."

I will CREATE a POEM so CHINESE oh you're off to see your sleeve of wizard

VI. Homosexuals with "outward characteristics of feminity—or lesbians with male characteristics—are often difficult to employ because of their effect on their co-workers, officials of other agencies, and the public in general."

Penetrate your layers lick those pores clean I am befuddled get on the tables the floor is lava

VII. Homosexuals who think they are discreet are, in reality, "actually quite indiscrete [sic]. They are too stupid to realize it, or else due to inflation of their ego or through not letting themselves realize the truth, they are usually the center of gossip, rumor, derision, and so forth."

Show me your seat of majesty your theory of beauty hell for you go to hell

VIII. Homosexuals who try "to drop the 'gay' life and go 'straight' . . . eventually revert to type."

Chanson de geste I creep on your friends' IGs to catch glimpses of you come on I'll fatten you up Hansel & Gretel

IX. Homosexuals are "extremely vulnerable to seduction by another pervert employed for that purpose by a foreign power."

Like a champion greyhound I'll run till my lungs collapse

X. Homosexuals are "extremely defiant in their attitude toward society," which could lead to disloyalty.

He is slow as molasses but burns bright as a hot plate thru oven mitts

XI. "Homosexuals usually seem to be extremely gullible."

Thinking abt David Beckham & his Minnie Mouse voice shush baby let me in

XII. Homosexuals, including "even the most brazen perverts," are constantly suppressing their instincts, which causes "considerable tension."

I am not perfect for example I sometimes have ingrown nails & eat so much lasagna my eyes seal shut

XIII. Homosexuals employed by the government "lead to the concept of a 'government within a government.' One pervert brings other perverts. They belong to the lodge, the fraternity. One pervert brings other perverts into an agency . . . and advance them usually in the interest of furthering the romance of the moment."

Children are taught how to ostracize they learn how to hate for example I know nothing abt sports but I hate Cleveland sports

We need a government where we don't have to depend on the mercy of bureaucrats or the kindness of strangers

Christen me with your loins as I salute death

POLO BLUE

Bootleg Siken, do you feel the same way abt me?
Do you laugh abt me with your little friends?

You're not like the other one, the blond—
The one who said *someday you'll work for me*

The courthouse steps, the flash of the camera
His corpuscle, his pomade, that lizard skin wallet (chartreuse)

How, in my mind, we were together yet
I was always a few steps behind

He is mayo—I don't eat mayo—
at least not anymore

Put your feelings in a group home,
buy me 99 roses, teach me to kiss down there

I want you real close, read Danez to me
Time for you to 出招, make your move

I'll break you down, sell you for parts—
I'm my own Tiger Mom, my personal Big Daddy

小夜灯 LITTLE NIGHT LIGHT

i'll be ur warm-up act

i'll be ur dirty rice

dutch oven means a mouthful of farts

men's packaging looks like it could impregnate me several times

most dudes mediocre

i fill u with adorations

the paul robeson of lovemaking

hapless

i show range like mariah

she is lady m

she love cake

sink u in sweetness

if tanagers were teenagers

don't be formulaic

go thru our daily circuits of wondering

i can't notice u cuz ur all that i see

tonight

we beat back the rains

7 x 12

^ ^

UR PATTER==UR AMBUSCADE

UR ABRADED==ALMOST FLENSED

MY DELICIOUS HAM==IT FLY

FLAWLESS DROP-KICK=='99

BEAUTIFUL MISTAKE==WE GOOD

FOREIGNER==BAND FROM ENGLAND

KISS ME MORE==SHINY FIXTURE

PASSEL BOYS==KISS PASTEL BOYS

U CUTE==LONE STAR GANYMEDE

HARD PORPHYRY==RED ROCKET

BREATHLESS==MOUTH VARIORUM

U ALWAYS==VADE MECUM

AREA CODE 886

she had a boyfriend named henry & i wanted one too
he waited for her after class & i wanted that too
subtle is not in my vocabulary (no free lunch)

//

wuz that fancy word to describe nostalgia
for something u've never experienced (desiderium)
anyway i swear i lived in late 80s taipei
right after martial law was lifted
made a living writing poems on postcards
not rich but i had a black mercedes

//

im haunting & powerful ur daring & strange
my intelligence so fluid & crystallized u wanna lick it
u say ur communist but ur swelling like colonial ambition
u may be an unfeeling capitalist but u really have a way wit words
i hope u don't take offense but ur dressed like the aga khan
i'll buy wut ur selling two in each color
everywhere u go u litter the world a trail of broken hearts

//

i know ur trying ur absolute hardest but i just can't get there
i think i overdid it wit the wiener schnitzel
u shouldn't have rubbed that lemon in my eyes
at one pt or another i could watch entire planets get obliterated & feel nothing
dead martians everywhere i won't even look up from my fkn cereal
ur throbbing in me like an underground poker game stop being judgmental

//

ariana reines stole our heirlooms tried to sell them back for five dollars
i refused, told her *i'm ur favorite poet's favorite poet*

//

if wut u give me is the same as wut u give everyone else
i don't want it (osmosis)

奢侈 LUXE

sky half-orange half-purple crushed velvet
fuck-u money walking lil dogs
snooty mumbling hostesses
flashy flamingos in faux fur
latchkey kid in a sable coat
toni collette chatting up sienna miller
they envy me & my stouffer's
either could play me in biopic
handsome guy getting stood up
double-fist those drinks sir
i'm chaste & this is a single-seater
au poivre means ur heat on my tongue
*if not all the others'
mediocre white men talking abt their legacies
u have no legacy
u'll be dead & gone before u hit the ground
forgotten before ur body is cold
fk ur beloved spurs
absent friends still here with us
hands on stems or cupped around bottoms
andy's ghost is laughing at u
the dogs bark but the caravan moves on
rich parents are essential 2 good writing practice
i like quiet luxuries like boys with black nails
brave & tall
boys who draw <3s in margins
our hands touching over & over
altering the course of the universe
when i think of sad moments ur there
when i think of happy moments ur there 2
funny how that works
i fix ur glare
u shine 2 bright
so cute i'll endure small slights & little indignities
spend 2 much time immersed in vanilla
ummmmm u could convince me of anything
seductive like a playlist with all my favorite songs
don't run out the clock
we should take this 2 the next level
i promise i am good at internet

香格里拉 SHANGRI-LA

To be honest with you, I just assume everyone speaks Chinese

What happened to that Scottish boy with the different-colored eyes ????

If trends are cyclical, is it time to bring back CHATROOM POEMS ????

You are beautiful like my manners

Crystals really do a lot to a room I want to eat on a pile of crystals

Please do not ask abt my self-care/writing routine b/c if I had one would we be here? I think not

My Chinese eyes are all squinty from zooming in on low-res poetry images

Premium content—Madonna told me to be good & I have exceeded expectations

Good evening to Logan Lerman ONLY

Haha Cavafy I wonder if he would have written abt me do you think he was into Azn

Sweaters are like hugs

Read abt Whitman "self-ghosting" & when I say I have a new kink—

RECENTLY VIEWED ???? I am still watching this ish

Stronger than I been before

My default setting is Azn Glow

Read 6.5 as 6'5" & that tells you all you need to know

They say find a job you love & you'll never work a day in your life. Well I love judging your shit I am like so judgy it's incredible

Attn universe I need to win some contests it is Chinese holiday so I can do whatever I want

What's your favorite non-sexual act of intimacy?—NAPPING ALONE

Look ma no hands

Some of you talk so serious abt manifestly terrible poems & I'm like hehe cheese

I miss swearing in public

PSA: talent is only minimally relevant. Dedication & discipline are much more important. See if Jessica Stam got the stamina, as they say

Chris Evans moderates & throws his shield at interruptions

If you made a horror movie, what extremely upbeat pop song would you want slowed down & creepified to play in the trailer?—Higher Love

Do crimes

Between this Viet Thanh Nguyen quote ("poetry, the least expensive of the literary arts") & Robin Coste Lewis saying she became a poet after suffering brain damage—I feel so validated

Eoin—you're like 75% vowels—daz hot

I don't use track changes my word is final

Phil of the Future is still cute. I wish you well in my future endeavors

A famous author said to me: with 3 words you have ruined this picture for me you really are a poet

My work being taught—I feel very powerful almost like D. A. Powell

My poetics is pre-outburst Galliano, 16 collections a year, Couture & Pre-Fall & Cruise & Resort . . .

My brave poetics putting hot sauce in a Valentino bag

Some poems b good but any number of ppl could have written them. Anonymous

These jobs really b tryin to get me to do work for free. No to "writing tests"—have you met me?

We are poet we have no land just cup noodle

I don't keep secrets I make secrets I necessitate them. I hate mini muffins

Great enterprise invent cranapple

Baked potato, 1962. I recall how, when asked to be nicer to R. Goodwin, Jackie said *but he's so ugly!*

Resting like a DOG! A SICK CUSTOMER!

Maybe iz like farewell tour. Maybe iz like animal going home to die

Thank you Russian giveth Chinese taketh away

I don't do trends but these pink & black covers are a trend I approve hunny

I don't know what load-bearing means but am admittedly intrigued

I'd be Patron Saint of Best I Never Had

Met a poet who said her fav books are Harry Potter I said yes yes very sad what has happened to Dobby

Need m*n to open particular jars but other than that drawing a blank

Every day I live in fear of being misidentified as another Azn poet but then I realize there's no one like me

Don't say my poems are uneven—daz your hairline

Writers, when you request a blurb, you don't need to frame it by saying how gross or terrible or whatever you are. We KNOW! TRUST!

Dog treat dat human also eat. If I read another poem with bone dust or marrow imma scream

I have the worst migraine after editing ms & this whiskey is not helping ???? I was told it would ????

Saw photo of tacos & said that is an excellent idea

Wonder if DC Madam is back in biz b/c Lady G has a flip phone so I KNOW they are not on apps

I have identified a startling queer cabal at a leading MFA program disturbing stuff they indoctrinate you how do I join

A construction worker, a m*nly m*n, wants to know what's so different abt my sex poems. Sir, I say, I am actually desirable in them. He weeps

Call me Costco b/c you need a membership & I am a lot to handle

Last week I resolved to reply "breakfast of champions!" to every email it has worked out remarkably well. Point is I am great at emails, prolific even, unless I am ignoring your ass

I just remembered a Senator who claimed to be a tech gal but did not know how to email

A poet tells me they listen to Chopin while reading my work. If you've read my poems, I don't foreclose the possibility that you've been naughty & skipped ahead, you will appreciate how hilarious that is

I am smol I am petite the Meowth of the team

Jane Hirshfield has a book called Cum Thief

We are poet we know what la petite mort is thank YOU!

OK WHO SNITCHED

A 货 (QUALITY FAKE)

"I feel good, I feel good / I blame you"—Paris Hilton

•

some say flashlight

some say fleshlight

to want is human

to flesh divine

hey this is a barnburner

your dumb traits, stupid attributes i couldn't care less abt

i read your horoscope first

some ppl aren't worth figuring out

russian doll of empty, eyeball you sweatpant season

you suck me in octopussy as portrayed by maud adams

i flail, fall into your melon mouth

see you later, agitator

you the prince of darkness, i the queen of sass

marilyn & the president, champagne taste beer budget

you're funny like swallowing dry ice

diversity doesn't mean one of each kind haha token

i don't mean to put a damper on your ambition

so talented the emperor would end you young

kill your career in fetal stage

your embouchure to my ambrosia

biceps swollen, ready to burst

legs pale, two thin lines planted in the ground

you quiver in your jockstrap

hold me like drink

our 默契, our vibe

o tacit understanding, o embarrassment of riches

you have no idea what you do to me

o how your teeth shine, o how am i supposed to fix this

带走你的垃圾 TAKE OUT YOUR TRASH

After this year, as assured as ONJ is Australian,

I'll never look at certain words the same way again:

"Q" . . . "Corona" . . . "Blake" . . .

I avert my gaze in the face of uncommon beauty

Simon says love me just a little while

Sometimes I want you next to me, but not in a sexual way

You're the church with the most loyal followers

so fiendishly devoted God takes a drag

asks *how'd you manage that?*

I tape a photo of Anna Wintour to my fridge so I eat less

I want your shiny armor . . . your thigh gap

your made-for-TV backstory . . . 8/7 Central

You suck eggs & sketch nudes

been alone so long your heart has bedsores

Fill me up like FAFSA, bear me much fruit

Gimme a tongue bath & thank me for it

Apart from me you do nothing

R u sure

No ur straight

I love it when you don't make sense

The last time I had arugula on a pizza

you were still alive

沙漠寂寞 LONELY DESERT

"What matters most is how well you walk through the fire"—Charles Bukowski

"Oui, il faut travailler, rien que travailler"—Rodin

•

le baiser de l'ange

my brain is swelling with great thoughts

i like skinny boys b/c i was a fat child

rodgers & hammerstein present

i am ur putz

forgotten like a blackberry ping

carillons are bells

take a seat rosa parks

i was a pleasure to have in class

i keep forgetting i don't need to see ur every post

u tried to tell kimberle crenshaw abt intersectionality

i am nice person u made me this way

MY MAIN DUDE IS A SHARK

"What do you want from me / I'm not America's sweetheart"—Elle King

•

bill knott called jane hirshfield a "bunter"
& one of two worst poets alive (the other was j. h. prynne)
there was a girl named wendy au i said *hey girl ur worth ur weight in gold*
my eyes are wide open but ur all that i see
i want to be trapped in a small space with u
ur so down on ur luck
i mean at some pt it looks like satire
don't u know
french ppl eat fried chicken cold
lumpy lumpy crabmeat
skate is fish
i hope ur pee comes out viscous
it'll look like molasses but there won't be aftereffects
b/c my heart is tender & tangled in ur fur
i'll undo the button on ur boxers
o mother-of-pearl
i promise i'll avert my eyes from hunks named daniel
i'm juicy steak ur carnivorous plant
call me ginger ale cuz i'll ease ur guts
where r u unknown allegory
i miss ur white-knuckled light-eyed goodness
relaxed like surf
u have ur own timeline
so vivid ur laugh
so sexual ur suggestion
ur confidence my homeland
for u i'll be pretentious like cornichons
relish in jellied animal parts &
little sausages on toothpicks
i said u were smoke & mirrors
u said *only mirrors*
i'll buy up all the mirrors in the world for u
i hope u'll be less alone then
like an arsonist u always return to the scene of the crime
i thought we were an item
i was half right i guess
ur a tool i guess
how dare u

ACQUA DI GIO

not the back of your throat

not this water & sand

but the bubbles

*

i'm so used to seeing your chest rise & fall

your pout your mouth elation

your lies make me feel so complete

*

i like them un poco eccentrico

maybe i can come visit you

& then we can never speak again

RASPBERRIES CAN BE TENDER TOO

fort lee, new jersey: birthplace of cinema

if i met you when hollywood was just desert

& there was no internet

would you have made the first move

no

not you with the premium calves

waste not your gym membership

you're not a star

you're a decent-looking civilian

your hair look like tail of beaver

no good

nope

something abt brass balls

something abt a monkey

painful excitement

domestic bliss

多久 HOW LONG

Friend of mine, they call him Pulpo cuz he's very handsy

Pulpo knows only one joke, says

SVA stands for Special Victims Academy

At which pt the bar breaks out in groans, says that's terrible

But he always leaves with the digits of at least one bird

(his words, not mine)

Pulpo gets into a bit of trouble in Thailand, evil spirits & whatnot

Long story short he has to trade a <u>SMALL</u> Warhol (roughly the dimensions of a big dick) to fix it

On the flight out of Bangkok he tells me his fav drink is vodka & Campari—just that—it's the flavor

The blood orange, the zest, most songbirds are male

Many poets appear to be heterosexuals

The genders, blues & pinks, vodka & gin

He is shaving & happiness is a warm gun

Why do all the monsters come out at night

Frankenstein is the doctor

Where's the farmer with the giant vegetables

We have that in common

I finally find out what "instrumental" means (no words)

Most poems should be no words

Most poems too long & too explainy

They turn my brain into mush

I hate them

冠军 CHAMP

"You are delicious I don't mind letting you know"—Frank O'Hara

"Why choose love / when hate comes first"—Carly Rae Jepsen

●

Why do cans still come with those plastic rings that kill dolphins & sea turtles & such

I thought we were past that in our post-racial society

Look at u

u stroke the ego

a flash of ankle

touch the id

a flare-up some would consider shocking

helpless shiver of recognition

a modicum of professionalism

savage truths coaxed from your precious mouth

demure as cut fruit

blond peaches bounce like they know the expense

We are modest dreamers (it takes a lot)

U like me better dressed as Wild Turkey

I like u better heartbroken

U taught me how to love at arm's length

Killmonger in a MAGA hat

I'm sorry I said to meet at Auntie Anne's

I didn't know ur parents were killed in a robbery gone wrong

Here have a pretzel

MARCO! POLO!

William Carlos Williams said *if it ain't a pleasure, it ain't a poem*

Kim Carnes fell in love with a poet

I want to write strange poems abt our pleasure

It's funny

I understand you more now than when you were around

I would visit your temple but I'm not exactly religious

I have noticed that you scrupulously update your website

It doesn't stress me out when you say that I'm perfect

I quite like it

I would give myself over to you so completely

Turn myself over like the proceeds of a crime

Let you hoard me like ill-gotten gains

If you believe that you probably think Snapchat makes cameras

& Uber is a transportation company

Poets love when things unfurl

Poets love things that clench like a fist

You're right

Pennsylvania is a commonwealth

You fuck me up

Heather Christle's alias is Heather Christie

Your poems suck

Don't name shit

Don't tell me the colors of things

You want some bath salts & Listerine

I want you to flip me duplex it lick the arches of my feet

Fuck me with your golden shovel

Think of Eleanor Roosevelt to keep from cumming

or is it Patty Hearst

a sensitive young man who committed war crimes & light treason

My screensaver is Taiwanese legislators fighting, throwing chairs, flinging shit

They lob water bottles, scream like they just learned how

Panda diplomacy is a thing

Don't piss China off

No panda no panda you're the panda

They'll snatch those baby pandas from your red-haired arms

Poets love when things fill with sleep

Poets love poems abt poeting as much as Hollywood loves movies abt Hollywood

I don't know what I want, I don't know if that depends on what you're willing to give

Your fragile ego likes it when I say I miss you

I like hearing from you

I am dumb

I pretend you don't exist

Blake: perfect, not William

Perfectly shiny & perfectly smooth

My heart swells

assuredly as rank hotdog water

I was going to poem a one night stand

Mayakovsky as curry restaurant

aspiring towards a condition of excellence

Guy I knew named Tom Skanke

pronounced "skanky"

a tragic typo led to a tragic end for our hero

wear nothing to the State Dinner but mascara & a splash of ranch water

Nancy Pelosi said *I don't hate anybody. I was raised Catholic.*

I love to hate

I am judgey as fuck

I am judging that word for not looking right

My love language is despair

Ok so where is this supposed Highway to Hell

You're the type to engage someone on the street abt Rwanda or Uighurs or Chinese encroachment

Sorry you expected Chang'e, goddess of the moon, no we aren't related

Sorry you thought you'd taste abalone & pearl, read abt silkworms & natural viagra

Sorry I can't name the planets, tell you the distance between the sun & the moon

Tindsay Lurner is not fucking clever

The only innovation coming out of the White House in the last 40 years is the button that summons the Diet Coke

& Joe Biden, being Joe Biden, Joe Bidening, got rid of that

大咖宣言 BIG SHOT MANIFESTO

"But sometimes what looks like disaster / is disaster"—Jane Kenyon

"It's like why am I even listening to you to begin with? You're a virgin who can't drive."—Tai Frasier

BIG SHOT MANIFESTO / yea you read that right / yea I'm 大人物 / A-list big shot / I see your sweatpant legs rolled up nonchalant / yea sprezzatura in my mouth / hahaha / forget bodies / I only want mango shaved ice / sweet syrup on my chin / coin in your mama's purse / yea I'm Protestant / yea fruit ninja / pay your dues / your face jacked-up / as welcome as lard in a coconut shell / can't cure stupid / 3 weeks ago I was just another f*g at Trader J*e's / now I'm drained pig's blood & machine-cut Lunchables / yea Blac Chyna blinking / *you're Beyonce & he's backup booty* / I hate buffalo anything / sneak me Canyon Pizza / your palm-grazing boy drizzle / I hope you choke on fish-oil pills / I didn't come here to dance / Hogwarts didn't have a school counselor & it shows / myth-harvested shrimp tamale / taco fishy real woman / lodged in my mouth like dreams / habits tender / feelings implied / miss that skin-to-skin contact / too many espresso shots & too much ruminating on my genius / clung like a weave / never ever waver / winter tango / grocery elves / blow your mind Ford Pinto / so elevated you're Eighth Day Adventist / think abt how guidebooks make tourist traps sound so fucking good / walk naked through the Louvre / like a ribbon of hallucinations / stalk Phi Phi Leh like Bond / overrated David Gandy hair / Aperol spritzes & BJs / none of that limp dick poetry abt clouds & angel dust / don't tell me "happy reading" you fuck / I read your stupid poem / I say stupid cuz it hurt my feelings / I sniff you out like Mori Kogoro / or maybe lose the plot / imbued with universal messages / Anyway your poem is very . . . detached. / Clinical. Removed. First-person but arms length. / There, there, you sick bastard / if you came out you could marry a nice Southern boy / raise some goats / watch him swell like a mango / show him your lip of understanding / his voice making your dick twitch / shake your bussy / strategic like the D.C. Sniper, see / dump him cuz he said "kilometers" / @michaelrcks my hater. This one [sic] for you baby. / you dirt fragment / spin that silk Jim Thompson / the curtains imperceptibly peach / part my legs ultraviolet / commune with tiny fissures / stuffed like Thanksgiving / OSS disappear like Thompson too / two of my exes live on lake washington boulevard / that's where cobain used to live / until he blew his brains out in the denny-blaine / red cheeks, grey eye-mask, milky plume / the pivotal moment / caught in your throat like stray dim sum / with fewer than 2000 in the wild & 400 in captivity, pandas are vulnerable to extinction / they are very difficult to mate in captivity / who r u / hemming-&-hawing hamlet on the hudson / u are a weed

I'm 城市猎人
CITY HUNTER

I'm 无耻
SHAMELESS

I'm 不切实际
IMPRACTICAL

I'm 真功夫
REAL EFFORT

万万没想到
NEVER THOUGHT

回到十年前的今天
TO GO BACK, 10 YEARS AGO TODAY

民国七十七年
THE 77th YEAR OF THE REPUBLIC OF CHINA

踩到地雷
STEP ON A MINE

大件事
BIG DEAL !

GIRL SLEUTH & BOY WONDER

Mr Thoreau aint shit to me　　—　　pop culture crassness my middle name
　　　　In death I cherish
　　　　　　a blanket & gun
　　　　　　　　woodsmoke & splashes
　　　　　　　　poems & ラムネ
　　　　　　　　　　onigiri in clear cellophane
　　　　　　　　　　& muskmelon in fancy paper
　　　　　　　　getting lost in cul-de-sacs

I want to be unhinged　　　　　　—　　Conjurer of sly magic ::
　　　　speak truth to power
　　　　　　　Sorry but I have standards
　　　　　　　　　bliss point & maximum glee
　　　　　You know who you look like?
　　　　　　Luther Vandross

I'll behave myself　　—　　avoid getting hate-crimed
　　　　it's ritual,　　　　　　　　wander the house
　　　　　　　　　　　　dodge shadows
　　　　　　call out the hacks
　　　　check in on acolytes
　　　　　　　　　　　　　　ponder the rule against perpetuities ::
　　　　　　　I won't neglect you,
　　　　　　　I promise

Stoned tigers as in high as in ganja　　—　　stumble over syllables
Currency of wit in this free market of wills
　　　　your money aint good for this　　速食爱情
Need you bad, scholarship based on meritorious skin color
　　　　I am what you call me ::
Chinese erasure
　　　　Jared Leto will never work in this town again

Homeroom angel　　—　　take me to church Snatch-22
　　　　Deep breath Shady Hawkins
　　　　　　summon up pretty crocodile tears
:: Seize empathy for the plague
　　　　trace bullet wounds with horrible edges
　　　　　　down drinks spiked with superstition
Convulse in that ghastly way　—　lips fading into mesquite
　　　　wrapped in bacon like all good things
　　　　　　Tantalus till the end
　　　(my fragile grapes)
　　　(flickering) ::

　　　　　　　　Can't wait to feel you again ::
　　　The revolution will be televised

59

Media as Opposition Party   —   Quaaludes & free rubbers
Little Spoon,   I'd rather die standing than live on my knees
        :: time wasted California waiting
                    admiring dunes & smoking that poverty grass
                    forgetting Manhattan &
Christmas at the St. Regis ::
                real classy & real ニューヨーク
        white tablecloths every square inch starched
                            chrome lamps with that special patina
steaks that cut above   waiter boys with toothy smiles
            & impossibly small waists,
black trousers washed one too many times,
        eyes twinkling *Eat the rich*
bodies a symphony *Fuck you pay me*

富二代
    山寨巴黎
        外貌协会
            煽风点火
            无可避免
                拌饭男神
                改邪归正
                    穿梭机
                    放大假

                                        —
                                    IS THE FUTURE
                                    CLEARER UP THERE?
                                    I NEED SOME GOOD
                                    NEWS RIGHT ABT NOW
                                    . . .

                                    I SWEAR I'LL KICK FATE
                                    IN THE FACE . . . I'M
                                    HOLY.
                                        —

GARDEN STATE TRICK

"*I want no smoke with the Chinese coz they are smart and quick*"—Cardi B

REASON IS TREASON / the act of letting a person into your home / involves: / yellow fever / caffeine tears / squirrels on jet-skis / white ppl calling 911 on lemonade stands / fireworks not flowers / cheese & mustard on rye / drunk owls (a "parliament") / mid-apocalypse / & a colony of mice / My Beard Papa mood / 谢谢你的肠粉 (thank you for the rice noodle rolls) / Little soul mighty griffin / I would die for u / u are so smol / I think we're alone now / Chinese belt & road / slit eyes in the moonlight / first sip of beer / kiss the rim / wait to spill our guts / am I too strong or too proud? / what's your room number? / I want you horizontal / spin me a salvation / I'll snuggle your worm / let the rabbits go / It's not you it's the locusts / the sugar cubes in my pocket / no harm no foul / sovereign citizen / Keystone State / 上海2004 (Shanghai2004) / searchlight over the valley / a listening lake / you the extra in your own movie / over-caffeinated & woozy / tortoiseshell glasses left in a cab long ago / fingers stained green with cash money / swallow that saguaro / the devil inside me / WANT that Miracle Whip / 死无遗憾 (die without regrets) / You the neurotic Valerio / ugly haircuts & empty pews / try to forget Anita Hill / stop folding my underwear / start wearing briefs / Call you Adnan Syed cuz you killin it / white faces on screens / fruit bats & astropastorals / Tamil word for fox's skull / pasivo mole / pushing rope / bowling shirts & barbeques / yea we need this beaver energy / unbutton your crotch / bag me a Yale boy / hold my beer cuz I seen them walking / shoot crows cuz they black / You're absurd / I'm obsessed / mild winter / light coat / straight hair slicked back / black tongue furious like parrot / climb into my life machine / that blue thing is what he washes his ass with / why is it so close to his mouth / put my lips on shiny ribs / spend my sweet inheritance / Capitalism with Chinese characteristics / they say it's not a mistake if you learn from it / so what have I learned from this / 自问自答 (lit. self ask self answer) (fig. rhetorical) / a New York 10 is an L.A. 5 / heartbreaking sunbursts vast & wild / offer orisons to Lovely Dude / *Kindness goes a really long way*, Lovely Dude says / Griffin Griffin Griffin —— muster some enthusiasm —— your varsity blues & Hollywood endings . . . ☺☺☺

PATRON SAINT OF LOST BAGELS

for evan
(#86 most popular boy's name)
you know who you are

i stiffen :: is it wrong that : thomas rhett gave me light crabs : charlie puth made that choking noise : nick jonas said to cover my face : is it right that

you are my :: war with loneliness : 30-day trial : rubber duckie in alligator-infested waters : undeserving love : made in china : love 1994 : per-my-last-email : cat's paw : beast of burden : little nap : long bath : second favorite : pure love idiot : brainwashed little prince : daily forbidden fruit : not-necessarily : winner-takes-all : better-than-you : eureka moment : hand of god : lucky draw : moonless night : moonlit pool : ghost ship : heavenly kingdom : weather of love : right as rain : hot 100 : lightning in a bottle : so close : so far : so what : faulty parachute : search for black box : sea to shining sea : kennedy curse : kennedy hair : whiteboy : branches of government : united states of : shit sandwich : past life : worth-waiting-for : chat a little : dance a little : charity lover : 10 seconds later : honeymoon suite : birthright prada : blacked out : red white blue : buzz lightyear : no. 0 : beef with broccoli : wild child : cheap love song : genius children 1985 : private tutor : spellcheck's worst nightmare : unhappy hour : 10 years later : lost love museum : love in the wrong universe : paris hilton : queen of jordan : tamil tiger : honeyed sun : black rainbow : dumpster fire : hungry hungry hippo : wonton : cheat day : question mark : dictionary : bible : red carpet ready : chillin with no makeup on : whereabouts unknown : every thursday : that-should-be-me : pumpkin carriage : pumpkin spice : september : june : december : watergate : still got it : cobwebs : crickets : human search engine : human decoder : japanese robot : one-eyed jack : loose sleeve of wizard : intern like alexander skarsgård : intern with huge dick : call me maybe : this time next week : goodbye : wawa cherry icee : some personal news : peach emoji : peach emoji : peach emoji

AREA CODE 604

. . .

. . .

"I will comb it with my own claws," said the dragon, "for I see that the child has hair the colour of gold, which is the only right colour for hair."—Travel Light by Naomi Mitchison

n.b. #1: that dragon is racist as hell
n.b. #2: this poem could be about anything you want
n.b. #3: how do you feel about a time-travelling consort finding love in a hopeless place

. . .

. . .

A whiteboy asks me to interpret his dreams
Why do I dream about my teeth falling out
I say it means you want me very badly
Another whiteboy heartbreaker asks what I do
I tell him I invented whiskey sours
I'm a sommelier for root vegetables
I run a book club for fans of One Direction
The screenwriter William Goldman said about Hollywood: "Nobody knows nothing"
He meant that even after a hundred-plus years of filmmaking
No one actually knows how to make a successful movie
Sure-things bomb & longshots win big
When it comes to us // nobody knows nothing

. . .

. . .

White people know all about the Stanford Prison Experiment
(Innocent) (An aberration) (For science)
But nothing about the Tuskegee Study
Or Wounded Knee
Or Chinese Exclusion
Or Japanese Internment
(Forget them) (They are yellow)
Karr was right to say: *plus ça change, plus c'est la même chose*
(The more things change, the more they stay the same)

. . .

. . .

White people who say they are "comfortable" really mean that they are richer than God
I find in your cabinet of bizarre curios
a delicate vial of four green leaves
Luminous, scalding, teasing, sentient, temperamental
Your lips ring with strange rain
Your tastebuds dance as I put myself on your tongue
My synapses sing like a suspect facing 20-to-life
You make me crumble // with your devastating gaze
Your dominant assertiveness meets my gentle yielding
Our labor of love

. . .

. . .

You make me giddy like I'm on horse tranquilizers
mess & quake // sting & salve
feeling my way through a dark theater
There is a house in Sumiyoshi-ku, Osaka
designed by Tadao Ando
with no exterior windows
because the owner wanted to feel
"not in Japan"
to compensate for lost light
an interior courtyard was created
In Japan "free size" means one-size-fits-all
Do you like my navy dufflecoat

. . .

. . .

Ecclesiastes said there's nothing new under the sun
but there is always new joy to be felt // new delight to be found
though it's hard to get excited about tomatoes
I memorized the riddles but not the answers // the tunes but not the words
You plant a flag // it's one of passion, rigor, ambition, collisions, kinship
Today, Madame President, we're all Adam & Eve & Steve

. . .

. . .

Whiteboy daddy longlegs
turn your face toward me
The face that could take a thousand lives
& murder me a million times

Belt loosened
You're immortal
You on top & me feeling weightless
Pimp my affections for
your flawed shine
your intelligent design
your pizza-burn sensitivity
your dirt road & no map
your conscious uncoupling
your fecund loins & imagination
your tongue darting around my danger zone
your practiced mouth intimacy
& your massive quiet glory
You watch me swallow, eyes wide open
With a serious expression, you say with absolute sincerity,
Uber but for trust exercises
. . .
. . .

BETWEEN TWO EVILS, I ALWAYS PICK THE ONE I'VE NEVER HAD BEFORE —Mae West

you were an omen afraid to be seen, replete with
disguises, cloak & dagger, master of camouflage,
committed & burning intensity, evading the gaze of
others, prevailing community standards, evolving
standards of decency, nervous around dump-trucks
& landfills, coarse walls & cruel thorns, pushing
yourself off a cliff, never waking up in time to greet
the morning rush, your feet killing you, god's dice,
squirrels with souls, gross strawberry yogurt, white
girls dying over spring break, whiteboys special,
especially the kind ones, you were a hedgehog &
i was a fox, i the multitalented one, you claimed
to do one thing well, i wondered what you thought
your one skill was, what does the fox say, double
consciousness, nurtured & cultivated, million-
dollar bonsai in a one-light town, lucille clifton said
that everybody needs both windows & mirrors in
their lives, mirrors to see themselves & windows
through which to see the world, miss lucille was
talking about race, you said our house didn't need
windows, because everything you desired was right
there, i wondered if this revelation meant you were
cheating, i said your best quality was between your
legs, distance frothed into wanting, the first cut is
the deepest, rubbing salt into the wound, deep state
totally invested in our love, all your base are belong
to us, neither snow nor rain nor heat nor gloom of
night could keep you from beer, wings, & fully-loaded
skins, religious, you rattled off the rules but broke
them, you possessed a photographic memory but
preferred to forget, sprawled out on my bed, looking
cute & vulnerable, lying through your teeth,

you had performance anxiety, sensitive, curious, &
voyeuristic, usually about my musculature, not sure if
i was more disappointed when you said hillbilly elegy
was a good book, or when you admitted you thought
ayn rand made sense, you said all of our love could
fit in a tiffany box, you meant this in a good way,
i said so can a turd, you kissed me, fighting for
attention, you said life boiled down to, what have
you done for me lately???, i laughed & laughed,
because you were the most generous person i knew,
unabashed, limitless, happily ever after

LE BAIN DE CRISTAL

rené magritte, circa 1946-49

. . .

. . .

Madame President

I rise today

Ass crack of dawn

An outfit that works

Jeter's not my dog, I just support him

I'm flattered when mistaken for a college student

I didn't realize ear candling was junk science

I don't know where my yearbooks have gone

I'm not writing about gun violence

Who wants to read about that?

I read the Wikipedia entries of scary movies

Like The Crow with Brandon Lee

What if you were trapped in an airline magazine?

Midwestern steakhouses, shitty sweatshop shirts

Conventionally-attractive whiteboys

The world is right there but you stay in Omaha

Boys love your wood sage & sea salt

Their heads whip around

They ask you to dance

Take that, Becky (or are you Karen now?)

It isn't healthy to dwell on how unresponsive Congress is

We all know Congress doesn't do shit

Yea it's completely captured by industry

I'd rather talk about my special interest in you

Your term-limit proposal is garbage

You'll have new people who can't even find the bathroom

& they're going to be equally corrupt

So you're really just trading a bunch of incontinent hacks for another

On Earth We're Briefly (Cherry Chapstick)

When I Grow Up I Want to Be a List of (Funny Azn Writers)

Someday I'll Love (White Rabbit Creamy Candy)

Edible Chinese paper soft & inoffensive

In your mind you've moved in with him

Living together in that Potemkin village

Your immigrant work ethic

Time waits for no man

You really like his
Big, uncut
Structural
Change
I like when whiteboy-Azn girl couples stare at me
With the full realization
That they have both
Narrowly escaped my clutches
Your poetry is pointless rambling
Your poetry is a screaming queen
Your poetry is evil poet Chen Chen
Let's instead have our pillowtalk about superdelegates
It's not colonialism
It's sadism
Forget hearts & minds
Why don't you follow your own advice?
People think politicians don't care because nothing ever changes
They're right
People think politics is elitist
Yea but clearly any buffoon can do it
People think party labels define someone's character
In this day & age, maybe
People think what they do matters to humanity
If you're rich & white, maybe
They say I write for dominant gaze
But
No
I write for subs too
Citizens United
No money no honey
Happy wife happy life
Mother's milk of poetry
You bloom
You ache
You want justice
Butterface Ansel Elgort folds me into origami
If we had an actual conversation
You would know that "anything"
means
"anything but Chinese"
No fats

No femmes

No Azns

No fun

You thought Oscar de la Renta still alive

You confused fugu (pufferfish) with fugue (????)

You mistook me for my Azn colleague

Haha jokes I have no Azn colleagues

So many poets are all doom & gloom

When there's a blackout, the murderers come out

It's that type of society

What do you want from me?

Her new bloke looks like partial birth abortion

The heart of a flea & the brain of a shark

Notable talent

Catch sperm with mouth

Culture warrior's manifesto

How to be alone

Dirty hustler

You are bent

Where are you really from

The future

Your English is very good

Yea & you look like Leni Riefenstahl cousin

You people are so smart

Yea just don't make me do calculus

Honeypot

Waiting for heartache

Fast love orange Play-Doh

Tangy despacito lime meringue pie

"Sweet is the memory of past troubles."—Cicero

Dear Sir or Madam

Sounds too binary

So are we back to

To Whom It May Concern

They parrot the talking points

They say the right lines

They make you believe

But it's a shell game

Just watch their hands

. . .

. . .

INTERNET BOYFRIEND

yea
charming but inconsequential
sorry we got a little too close
a little too familiar

don't u sometimes feel
like a dog
who shat
in the wrong place

///

look at u
so shiny with fullness
if this is a con
it's time to make the ask
rob me
steal from me
take all my money
sell all my possessions
make me suffer
have me feel torment
leave me destitute
then at least i can say
for one brief moment
i was what u wanted

HARDCORE HAPPINESS

They say good things come in 3s, like the Powerpuff Girls & celebrity deaths. I've lived in 6 homes (maybe 7, possibly 9, I forget) on 2 continents. I'm very good at talking to ppl, even ppl I don't like. I grind them down with my witticisms. I think that is why strange men shout *grinder* at me . . . is it my fault I'm habit-forming? Is The Taking of Pelham 123 now considered a nostalgic movie?

* * *

You keep your heavy watch on during sex,
bulk on little wrist
I put a hand on your stomach,
hear the words mingle, gurgling
You take a fistful of hair, push your bangs back
You have jowls like Anjelica Huston
(not pronounced HOW-stan like the street)
(at least I don't think so)
You watch my innocuous love desires,
let me admire your L.L. Bean, your Cold War antics
It's all in the name of fun—
—I suppose

* * *

If a mysterious name enters your ear, you best not repeat it
If you need a name to sweetly cradle, choose mine
If you need hands to stain with red & black lacquer, use mine
If you need animals to wait for, hold my stained hands
If you need dreams to cloak your eyes, shroud them in mine
If you need mist to fill your lungs, take a deep breath—
—pretend we have not yet been born

* * *

O avarice
O finest sea island cotton
I've always wanted to meet someone falling from a ladder
Yellow Rose of Texas, a whore edging me
Caftan of the finest silks known to man
I say *man* deliberately here
God is present in beauty
Like how I am inside you
No, hold on
Like the Senate I'm just 1 of 100 to you
It's okay, don't exert yourself—
—I don't go after stuff that seems too good to be true

VOYEUR

He weeps silently, gaily,

listening to Simon & Garfunkel.

Some days he is happy.

* * *

Hey Danielle

You are nobody

You equivalent to nuked coffee

Some warmed-up tuna casserole

* * *

Some people are happy with some bread some cheese

Give me some dijon at least

Or don't—

—which is what happens

THE LAST ORGY

I

We're all good
I say to the waiter eye-banging me
as my date curls his lip

II

You're so chaotic
i am
but so r u

Your pen name Jean Christmas
strange thing
that's legally binding

III

Hey
you
looked
so good
2
me
@
the last orgy

IV

I wish I were someone who could hold your attention
—must be nice!
Doesn't matter now!

SOLITAIRE BOYS FOLLOW ME

-

-

As my head is bowed over meatloaf, I see God. Damn it, I think, should've gotten wings. Dude, I tell God, I've had a really long day. I make a mental note, the world is a mess but his hair is perfect.

-

-

He stands there, all musk & indecision, looking like he never misses a session of SOULCYCLE, figuring out how to love me. After much thought & prayer, he feeds me bacon & heart disease. It feels like home, truly, as the color drains out of my ROADRUNNER sweatshirt. I confess, I don't know how to make the prophecy better.

-

-

God fastens himself to my body, we are wild horses running in tandem, poppies in his opium war. Sugar, I say, don't worry. I don't need anything from TIFFANY. He looks relieved.

-

-

Sometime later, I spot him holding court at LITTLE CAESARS, my invitation conspicuously lost in the mail. Another time, he's papped on the Spanish Steps in his burnt orange polo, arm around a blond boy named Jasper.

-

-

BETRAYAL, 背叛, REWIND, 倒帶

-

-

I leave God a voicemail. Tell me how you want it, I plead. Love begets jealousy begets hate begets love begets nothing left. I hope I remember not to die in worship. Problem is, I don't want to sleep alone.

TAKE ME TO YOUR LEADER

"The echo / the two bodies no / sound at all"—Frank Stanford

::

Boys are like potatoes
I like them many ways
I pick them up at the farmers market
They come in all shapes & sizes
Scalloped so creamy & thin
They like to lounge on my couch after we do the deed
Their belts hanging undone
They're hard on the outside & soft once u loosen them up
U slide ur thumb into them
Their insides velvety sweet, inviting as a warm pond
Buggery good with any topping
Always better with sour cream, some chive
Boys are like potatoes
I like them many ways

::

Captain Morgan gave him an order he had to obey
. . . an offer he couldn't refuse
. . . drink

::

ur acute angle im hypotenuse

ur first class im stowaway

ur so hot they invented free refills for u

im burp ur cold beer

drink up

DEWEY CHEATEM & HOWE

no such thing as an artist w/o ego , just put the ego to good use

make sure u remember the little ppl , account for their inane suffering

i stroke ur ego , she cries hideous tears

ur just flat soda , no dance on my tastebuds

ur beard my faithful companion , roughness under fingerpads

i hold ur flag , u hoist ur petard

forget the root word , give me the root

mermaid laid bare , razor clams sichuan style

awful chinese takeout , brown sauce so delightful in its awfulness

ur the cutest in ur family , daz like being atlantic city's best casino

crooks & their watches , it's a heist

balaclava & baklava , he has a suitcase that he leaves behind

absolutely diminished , weighed against ur body

time doesn't heal anything , that's another lie they tell u

shifting as u uncross ur legs , fool's gold but i'll still touch it

u come unexpected as a sunburn , on top of a blueberry

o five-pointed star , pretty boy we are the same

there are no stars in hell , i should know—i was there

shit-stain/worm-brain gatekeepers , still overly interested in white happenings

most poetry is "white happenings" , predictable as seasonal allergies

most love poems just fkn terrible , one root canal after another

fruit most fragrant before it spoils , what have u done to my melons

爱情抗体 LOVE ANTIBODIES

///

conquer me glorious swordfish, your farts are kind of wet, unwanted like the last seat on the titanic, i wish life were simple like police procedurals, 24 mins & you know who the killer is, i saw a show that revealed the killer in the first few mins & worked backwards from there, it didn't last very long, that show, prob b/c our minds have been programmed to expect a certain run-of-show, the regular way things are supposed to go, so to speak, speaking of minds, aren't they supposed to frighten you, so haunting, those things, i guess we'll find out if you have that killer instinct, high school sweetheart, vouchsafed by heaven, show me how you kiss, that would be thrilling, wouldn't you say?

///

describing a melon as "strawberry red" is miscegenation
what u call cows chew
macerated no masticated
don't misconstrue it

is it true what they say abt horses
that they're really good at kissing
i wouldn't know
but u look like u would

wrap my pianist fingers around thick
garlicky sausages so berkshire pork
ah my inheritance
has beguiled yet evaded us for so long

///

Yes

You totaled your Infiniti trying to catch up to me

Ummm

Colors are important to flowers (some would argue essential)

No

The insistent tug of your sexual anesthesia

Maybe

Look at you such a nondescript eggshell white

MISSHAPEN ECLOGUE

\   u say victor hugo. halston's lover
\   passionate. a window dresser in the truest sense
\   was also famously well hung
\   yea. "also"

\   what am i supposed to do w. a big dick. no personality
\   slice it down the middle. serpentine
\   toss it in lemongrass. some chilies. hissing
\   throw it in a jar of embalming fluid. sheer

\   it will take years for u to go away. flawed
\   worse than a plastic bag. thin
\   someday u'll be a thing of the past. soft
\   like hanson. the osmonds. destroyed by flowers

\   u dare show up. whip at ur side. earth
\   desirous of heaven. ripe
\   we dream of heavy snow. broken
\   she gives u a gift. i give u the whole sleigh

\   u curl up next to me. loose
\   little smirk on ur face. drifting
\   where i end—u begin
\   where u end—i begin

孤单芭蕾 LONELY BALLET

how cold
indurate

how remote
oneiric

soy boy
what's not to love

ur words
my life force

my scruples
fit in the tiniest box

i write the world's worst love poem
unrivaled in its lack of imagination

the new boys
tireless as seals

so warm & excitable
stoked! even

u fling the glass
i find the courage not to get up

there u are
the ugliest kennedy

right outta central casting
that means white

gore invent internet
gwyneth invent yoga

froufrou
hausfrau

u promise me the whole enchilada
all flavor no grease

u know u have to tell me
if u are police

PATCHWORK CHECK

. : . Story goes

Boy wakes up utterly convinced abt provolone   Provolone the only thing on his mind

He knows provolone will fix his broken clock

bring the duckling back to life   unhatch the three eggs   take care of his chores

reassure the flowers, the bees   uncarve the tree

unvandalize the corner store   refill his orange soda

light the path   send the angels away   lead his balloon back to earth

He proceeds, cautious, soul starving for provolone he strongly suspects will

unanger the Karen   unbruise his cheeks   unsay the slurs

unsentence the accused   unmelt the icebergs   undo the elegies

shut Pandora's box   unwind every influence   reunite One Direction

Boy's eyes hurrying   he searches high & low   far & wide

shelves & cupboards & drawers   glide open & click back into place

Quietly Boy says *I want provolone*   *I want to taste nothing*   *until further notice*

*

You sicko   You kinda pretty   You give me form rejection

You are bad news   You are red flags   You give me big envelope

You are rose-tinted glasses   You are sugar cookie   You shiny boy

I can't believe I dedicated a poem to you   I am compliment veteran

My turn to pop your cherry . : .

DEAR ANDRE

It's been a while

That is to say, this is my first time writing

Obama said "no new friends" when moving to the White House

Trying to avoid the Clinton fate, the revolving door of hangers-on & hacks

A solid plan, except Obama's old friends include Valerie Jarrett of all ppl

Valerie Jarrett, who asked her WH staff to prepare talking points abt how wonderful she was, & her staffers couldn't think of any examples

The sheet said: (need examples)

But I digress, Andre, you've been on my mind a lot lately

You've run into some money troubles

You would think, after 40 years in fashion, you'd have a nice nest egg stashed away

But, no, you're on the cusp of eviction from a house you do not own

A house you say you own, except your landlords have been trying to kick you out since March 2020, right when a pandemic was happening, think abt that

We're in this mess b/c of a convoluted arrangement you supposedly had with your friends of 40 years

Until Edward Enninful took the helm at British Vogue, you were the highest-ranking black editor in history

Like ever!

You were friends with Andy & Mick & Bianca & Jean-Michel . . . everyone worth knowing

You were Diana Vreeland's protege, her favorite, & later a favorite of Anna Wintour's & Karl Lagerfeld's

You were valuable to Vogue b/c of your close relationship with Karl, though your relationships with both of those entities would eventually implode

But, yes, 40 years in fashion . . .

You waded through the muck, surviving ugly rumors abt sleeping around to advance your career although you were celibate

Clara Saint, YSL's publicist, called you Queen Kong

Your weight ballooned & you took to wearing gorgeous caftans custom-made for you by the likes of Tom Ford & Miuccia Prada

Anna Wintour used company money to send you to a fat camp—not once, but twice

You declared bankruptcy twice in your native North Carolina & once in New York State

But you held your head up high throughout, naively believing that hard work would get you places, that the American Dream was real

You believed this despite growing up in the Deep South, in an era that was less friendly than it is now

In fact, you were committed to the South, in retirement helping SCAD elevate its profile in higher education, bringing the biggest names to sleepy Savannah, Georgia, luring them with awards & accolades—now doesn't that sound like a beautiful thing?

I will always remember how you told me to do my homework

Just as you told the Oxford Union: *Do your homework*

When I tell my students some variation of this they always laugh, snicker

I don't know if this is b/c I am Azn & they are whites

It's a simple statement, to do your homework, meaning to study what came before, to know your place in the constellation of artists, to know whose shoulders you stand on, history, giants, etc.

I apply this to my poetic practice

But back to your friends,

You did so much for them, didn't you?

You never did a shoot at Vogue w/o shoes from their brand

You helped put their shoes on TV & in movies, told your celebrity friends abt them when they were unknowns

Your friends of 40 years, it started out okay, you were having money problems, couldn't get a car

So they bought one in their name & you wired them the money for it

This was when you still had income, horrible credit, but at least you had some cash flow going

Later you had mold issues in your apartment in the city & had to find somewhere to live

You saw a handsome house in White Plains & decided you needed to possess it, an impulse familiar to those of us who like beautiful things, this desire, this want

I have often wondered what drew you to suburbia when you are imprinted in the minds of so many as a city dweller

Someone who conquered New York City despite the odds, a trendsetter, someone inextricably tied to the city's unique celebrity ecosystem, glitz & glamor & *class*, not like the gauche & in-your-face Hollywood types

You decided to move to White Plains, this is when the seeds of trouble were planted

B/c of your terrible credit, we talked abt this earlier, you had your friends buy the house for you

Let's say the house was $1 million

Make it easy for me, I'm a poet, I'm bad at math, yea, Azn jokes abound

You enter into a lease agreement with your friends (it sounds like a bad idea already)

You say that the understanding is that you would pay your friends varying sums of money, & when that amount reached $1 million (i.e., the cost of the house), your friends would sign over the title to you

Abt a decade passes, by now you'd been fired from Vogue & your friends had lost their lucrative license (& thus were facing money problems of their own)

The lease agreement you originally signed lapsed a few years before & was never renewed, thereby converting you to a month-to-month tenancy

You continue to make sporadic payments in varying amounts, but you know, cash flow is a problem for you these days

Having said that, you've made abt $1 million in "rent" & other such payments, but now your friends are kicking you out, claim you owe more than $500k in rent

Shock! They've filed with the local court to evict you, they need money very badly, & want to sell the house

You know how fashion ppl are, they make $30 & spend $100, not very Azn

I think you'll lose your case, Andre, sad to say

Ppl are claiming that you're lying through your teeth, Andre, that no one would be so stupid

But you were useful to your friends-turned-landlords, once upon a time, so it wouldn't be too surprising for them to make concessions in the moment

But ppl insist that aspects of your story don't pass the smell test, just don't add up

They don't understand fashion, how ppl are paid pennies but have access to the most dreamy & fantastical spaces & holidays & freebies & swag

Like you they have no money in the bank & then they find themselves too old, or too fat, or too pregnant, or too tied to previous management, or disfavored for some reason, it's so unfair!!!!!

When the music stops they are left with nothing, their ass in the ground, which is exactly your predicament now, 72 & on the cusp of experiencing homelessness, backstabbed by ppl you thought were close companions, bad boys for life & all that

The lesson here is to always have things in writing, put it in black & white, you don't need to be a lawyer to know that

I'm sorry, Andre, I really did intend for this to be a poem abt friendship, but it's turned into a bitter little document with an unhappy ending—

I didn't mean to disappoint, to detail your friends' betrayal so vividly & in such brilliant language, my obvious poetic skill really coming to the fore like a blazing light, to expose your warts in this way—

Ah, well, does that finally make us friends—

SOMETHING ABT THE PRICK

ur words so heavy so good

i can only read a bit at a time

like ant lifting cake

u must be british b/c ur so extra u

i notice even when ur not around

i love u brett

*blake

let's get into a fistfight

show me apollo's belt

i'm a mama's boy

ur jacob's ladder

u couldn't get elected dogcatcher

or even county commissioner

come be my bunny

i will feed u carrots

brush the greasy hair from ur bloodshot eyes

come be my bunny

frantic & off-white

MONEY TREE

You always confuse *ladies' fingers* (as in okra) with *ladyfingers* (as in the biscuit)
Like why would they put okra in tiramisu

If you think "emperor of ice-cream" is pretty clever
read my poetry, get on this hamster wheel of greatness

If corporations are persons
we'll take them down to the Piggly Wiggly

Install some spikes on Lady G's fainting couch
Unleash angry albino peacocks

We'll send baby mice up their spines
smother them with a thousand bunnies

We'll play loud music, starting with Britney
make them study for the SATs, then the MCATs

We'll suspend them in KY
feed them the worst flavor of jello

We'll make them beg, cry out for Karen Pence
They want rights but won't pay the freight

I know this framing is deeply problematic
Pay-to-play, status quo & all that

I don't think you should pay for rights
But I want corporations to pay thru the nose

No, not just their "fair share"
Living is hard & I want everything

We'll take their savings, raid their shelters
Exchange it for bitcoin, spread the love around

Corporate personhood you get the shaft
Corporate persons this can be our little secret

I ALREADY LOVE MICHAEL CHANG

don't call me canal street ocean vuong
i said don't

oh u look so skin & thin & bones
like dog with tennis ball i won't let u go

amid the chatter of locker room talk, ridiculous "men's humor"
u look like everything that ever mattered & that will ever matter

do u want to crawl into & live inside an animal carcass or r u not a poet
nothing to halt the character of ur bathetic self

i want to be beautiful for u
no poem with the phrase "lover's bed" has ever been sexy

am i to understand that roaches love marijuana
poets luv balms & salves—how much r u hurting? (a lot)

quit the jibber-jabber & put ur mouth on mine
tadpole in my bosom

u seed & slip
this is a donut shop & ur herpes is triggering

copernicus was a nazi
u want tommy pico's pico

unremarkable as a sedge
forget the tempera of sky & sea, bring out the tempura

i piggyback off ur quickfire wit, ur turn of phrase
pretend to like philadelphia

try to overlook ur small cock
i'd rather run someone over on the schuylkill than be with u

being alive is a traumatic experience
is dehydration real

i have a sponsor for when my bf doesn't text me back
i'm the heir of a great american family

the weird thing abt complaining abt everything & complaining abt nothing
how none of it really matters

who'd u rather . . . channing tatum or president truman
voice of a generation

my kissing u & other acts of mercy
my boy victor he has the spoils

"flyover country" the worst slur u'll ever hear
objectionable like cubes of watermelon—$12 for 6—cut all uniform-like

he said his favorite poet was matthew d*ckman or the other one & i said dis is over
don't trust m*n & most definitely not the ones with thin lips

they bring forth the ching chong
pardon my candor

i'd rather be forward than backward
i serve lewks & god in that order

godsend—everything is relative
kissing u is like kissing me

u stifle
i stymie

ur lies ring so true
build me an ark, two of each kind

ppl living their lives, as they r prone to do
yea i clocked dat

ur poems pulling wings off a moth
ur words singing themselves off the page

when i read ur poems i am filled with self-loathing
b/c i wish i wrote them (b/c i wish they were abt me)

essex hemphill was right
everytime we kiss we confirm the new world coming

i'll give u something to write home abt
or ur money back

HUSTLIN' POPPIES

[   ]
TIGER BEAT
BACKSTAGE PASS
[   ]
A ROARING FIREPLACE
VOICE SORT OF HUSKY
[   ]
BRIGHT MUSCULATURE
ASSCHEEKS LUXURIOUS
[   ]
STONED
OR VAGUELY IMPRESSED
[   ]
UR SPARKLY
UR VIBRATING
[   ]
U HAVE A SILVER LINING
KING ME LIKE MUFASA
[   ]
U TELL ME U'VE BEEN RANSACKED
FOR LOVE & DICK
[   ]
"FIRST READERS" ARE OVERRATED
I WANT TO BE UR LAST READER, THE SOLE REMAINING PERSON WHO READS U
[   ]
DISTANCE KEEPS U SAFE
MAXIMIZE THE DISTANCE BETWEEN U & _____
[   ]
THE RARE TIME I WANT TO FEEL SMOL & CONTAINED RATHER THAN INFINITE
MAYBE IF I STOP PEDALING IT WILL COME

STILL LIFE WITH SUNGLASSES AT NITE

"I am not empty; I am open"—Tranströmer (tr. Patty Crane)

•

whiteboys at meijer

boisterous & bare-chested

the familiar procession like rows of corn

or an affirmative-action protest

or deleted body-cam footage

the chosen one

reverse racism! in the flesh

opens like a fan

he gives in w/o violence

buys me vitaminwater & a pet lobster

reads a poem referring to mt. fuji as—simply!—fuji!

it makes me laugh, fuji like last-name-only boys

their flanks hard & shapely

he puts some cheese on a nice plate, makes it taste good—presentation is everything

we consummate our love after watching the 2013 documentary blackfish

i am briefly his stooge, we harvest the purest form of love

he smiles tight as a muzzle, grins only make sense on white faces

need to break this all-or-nothing habit

you know what they say

white ppl masters at self-hypnosis

tall boys need bigger coffins

APOLOGY TWO WAYS

there's always a cute one & his shorter friend

no matter where you go

_____ want to know abt your friend your friend your friend

& what are we? chopped liver

baby are you molting? come back

we can be better than ever before

meanwhile

that downy trail of hair leads to devastation

SUNDAY POEM

he knew about saltwater taffy which is to say he knew red swimsuit & jersey shore which is to say ok boomer which is to say i was today years old when i learned this which is to say if a joke is told on SNL is that the kiss of death which is to say i listened to your most controversial food opinion which is to say pretty green eyes that forgive which is to say it's cuffing season which is to say too handsome to be taken seriously cedric diggory which is to say kill the spare which is to say urgent & necessary which is to say joe biden is one of us which is to say he knows the cost of a gallon of milk in 1978 which is to say sending a kid to college in 1980 which is to say sending a kid off to war in 1990 which is to say i stand with joe because which is to say he stands up for the pharmaceuticals & wall street which is to say somewhere in my car which is to say daring & vital voice which is to say don't pull your punches which is to say 明察秋毫 which is to say know your references which is to say we deserve to laugh which is to say we deserve to be entertained which is to say "doorwalkers" which is to say i thought you said "dogwalkers" which is to say "extra men" which is to say "confirmed bachelors" which is to say polite society which is to say bill blass & charles addams & norman mailer & halston which is to say valentine to ___ which is to say the same conversation swimming in my head which is to say my mother would've named me victoria if i were a girl which is to say gramsci said history teaches but has no pupils which is to say i admittedly don't feel as angry (?) as i should about billionaires buying the election which is to say don't revoke my progressive card which is to say any of them would be better than #45 which is to say except tulsi gabbard which is to say bloomberg is problematic but semi-competent which is to say buttigieg gets mad when challenged & his face puffs up & he has zero support with people of color which is to say does he even love chasten which is to say kamala should be catching fire which is to say klobuchar is a nutjob plain & simple which is to say she was shaking like a leaf which is to say midwest means white which is to say that's disqualifying which is to say who's our standard-bearer which is to say what about post-heart-attack bernie which is to say do the debates matter which is to say warren has a plan for that which is to say god laughs ha ha ha which is to say tattoo sleeves on lean beckham arms which is to say brooklyn which is to say play him like a ken doll which is to say am i supposed to find adam driver attractive

SORRY IN ADVANCE

i put these secrets into skin   fry them till they are golden brown

drizzle plum sauce on them   sweet & savory

       that is how they want me to write

instead   i write about timothée chalamet

•

some days i wake up & think i am nat wolff   or a little pig named wilbur

my governing principle is optimism   possibility loud & clear

       why are other people so dark so traumatic so sad their poems are like

abandoned trailer teeth claws death rape grease jet fuel blood gasoline walmart train tracks
bodies animals coyotes ravaged etc

       my poems are like

dom pérignon corn chowder lobster thermidor montauk dunes beach-reads oliver peoples two
hands coffee decaf is hell etc

if i have to hear about your infected hoof or how he let her flirt when you were ***right there*** again

we will have a problem   words will be exchanged   i will hurt your feelings

after all   i haven't forgotten   that time you read my work   & asked

       did amy tan write this

•

when you admitted you were one of the deplorables   i thought ugh   it's always
the cute ones

       & pushed your head down some more

MONTAGE WITH EXES

ur a triple threat like awkwafina

ur lies my sustenance

ur perfume my poison

tell me how u crave love

ur cult of no-personality

husks of boys, formerly young kings, in silent worship

they kneel, backs turned, hands empty

u mistake them for stone angels in a garden

or ghost maps on funny paper

they fall, catching themselves, glint of white roses swaying

the room rendered a void, there will be no shot of recognition

i could not save u from urself

but do not despair

let's try this again

THE BOG TURTLE IS NEW JERSEY'S STATE REPTILE

so : so : ur extraordinary :

like a sunset caring what comes next

ur the prince who makes it thru the forest

body unscathed : pretty face untouched

thank god for photosynthesis

i spray ur cologne on my knuckles : smell u on my fingers :

any ol' plant won't do

we make grunting noises : ppl stay away

u leap : lose ur stripes

some things u can't ever publish

white ppl would sooner notice bush & thistle than see us :

that's how i lived in the american for 7 days

which got me thinking :

i want to hang out on a cloud with u :

somewhere undisturbed & unfound

the two of us : there : unmarked :

not blinking at all :

no one ever treat u so right

CONCERTO: ONE THING LEADS TO ANOTHER

"Darlin', in your wildest dreams, you never had a clue"—Quarterflash

•

a frock, gold thread, white trim like a stab of light
pony-hair slippers, prim & proper

i know i was passing notes to u in class
but for the life of me i can't remember what they said

confucius was confused
the body needs rest & jesus

the only thing i've lost is my mind
too perfect a memory—too much of a good thing

u remember all the slights & hiccups & blemishes
the deepest cuts & the hardest words

mo'nique said real womxn sacrifice
so harden ur heart (i am)

i insist on calling it "airbb"
even lawyers click thru service agreements w/o reading

what would u fit in a snowglobe
a nice town, farm animals as glorious pets

the only thing i'll butcher is pronunciation
may or may not be sexual but who's to say

counterintuitive but i would love to fit a safari in mine
safaris r not okay irl but permissible in the context of a snowglobe

i think i like cheetahs
lightning bugs & fireflies r the same creature

ur two parts fuccboi one part imitation soy
ur department store i'm bodega

i give u rhyme—u give me reason
who r all these ppl

DUCK DUCK GOOSE

i like european boys b/c then i know exactly why i don't understand them

nah, that's just something i say

lift ur shirt

flash us ur skin

release those fluids

i don't know abt exit wounds or the night sky

i'm more concerned with entering shit

ur a maze i'm stuck in

i get into situations w/o figuring how to get out

ur a lot more than infinity

funny how ppl say until their heart stops they will do this or that

seems like too much responsibility for a heart

isn't it typical for a poet to ruminate over the heart's importance

as if it were some mechanical device working in fits & starts

i guess it's really game over when the widget stops

u serial dater with emails out the wazoo

yea that explains these sticky fingers & why ur mad at me

but hang on

i smell u on my pillow even tho u've never been here

tell me this: who is riding michael knight

& r we the future of poetry?

ENVOI

I don't want a life of meaningless, casual associations
I want all of ur meaning, all of ur associations

ACKNOWLEDGMENTS

With ample gratitude to:

Librarians & teachers everywhere (look at me now) ...

- - -

The Poetry Project at St. Mark's Church for awarding its Brannan Prize to me ...

Cedar Sigo had this to say in his judge's citation:

I chose these poems for their film-like flow and beautifully encrypted collisions. I love how this voice seems hell-bent on talking back to our captors. It can move from wet and lush to syllabically strict almost instantaneously. Our times have been shrunken down into glimmering, twisted artifacts that demand to be sounded out ...

- - -

Lambda Literary, for its support & confidence in having me edit & creatively direct the 2020-21 EMERGE anthology ...

- - -

My beloved blurbers, for their friendship & taste ...

- - -

Jason Zuzga, for his brilliant contribution ...

- - -

The editors at Another New Calligraphy/Impossible Task; Broadkill Review; Burrow Press; The Cortland Review; Cream City Review; The Florida Review; The Laurel Review; The Liminal Review; The Meadow; Minnesota Review; Nashville Review; No Contact Mag; Pidgeonholes; Santa Clara Review; The Shoutflower; & Sinking City Literary Magazine, for their fine selections ...

- - -

The incomparable CLASH team ...

- - -

& everyone who has supported me along the way & in the future!

ALSO BY MICHAEL CHANG

Drakkar Noir
Chinatown Romeo
Boyfriend Perspective
Synthetic Jungle

MICHAEL CHANG

MICHAEL CHANG (they/them) is the author of several collections of poetry, including BOYFRIEND PERSPECTIVE (Really Serious Literature, 2021) & the forthcoming SYNTHETIC JUNGLE (Northwestern University Press, 2023). Tapped to edit Lambda Literary's Emerge anthology, their poems have been nominated for Best New Poets, Best of the Net, & the Pushcart Prize. They were awarded the Poetry Project's prestigious Brannan Prize in 2021, & serve as a poetry editor at the acclaimed journal Fence.

ALSO BY CLASH BOOKS

GAG REFLEX
Elle Nash

WHAT ARE YOU
Lindsay Lerman

PSYCHROS
Charlene Elsby

AT SEA
Aïcha Martine Thiam

THE SMALLEST OF BONES
Holly Lyn Walrath

AN EXHALATION OF DEAD THINGS
Savannah Slone

WATERFALL GIRLS
Kimberly White

ALL THE PLACES I WISH I DIED
Crystal Stone

LIFE OF THE PARTY
Tea Hacic-Vlahovic

GIRL LIKE A BOMB
Autumn Christian

THE ELVIS MACHINE
Kim Vodicka

SEPARATION ANXIETY
Janice Lee

INTERNET GIRLFRIEND
Stephanie Valente

HEHEHEHE
G.G. Roland

AN ACTUAL PERSON IN A CONCRETE HISTORICAL SITUATION
Blake Middleton

SHITHEAD LAUREATE
Homeless

WE PUT THE LIT IN LITERARY
clashbooks.com

 @clashbooks  @clashbooks  /clashbooks

Email
clashmediabooks@gmail.com